SAMMY'S EXCELLENT REAL-LIFE ADVENTURES

Titles
in
A Seeking Sammy Book
series:

*Sammy's Fantastic Journeys
with the
Early Heroes of the Bible*

*Sammy's Incredible Travels
with
Jesus and His Friends*

*Sammy's Excellent
Real-Life Adventures*

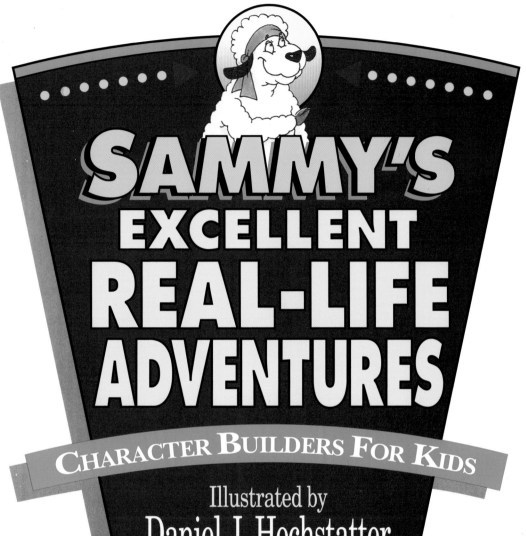

SAMMY'S EXCELLENT REAL-LIFE ADVENTURES

CHARACTER BUILDERS FOR KIDS

Illustrated by
Daniel J. Hochstatter

THOMAS NELSON PUBLISHERS
Nashville

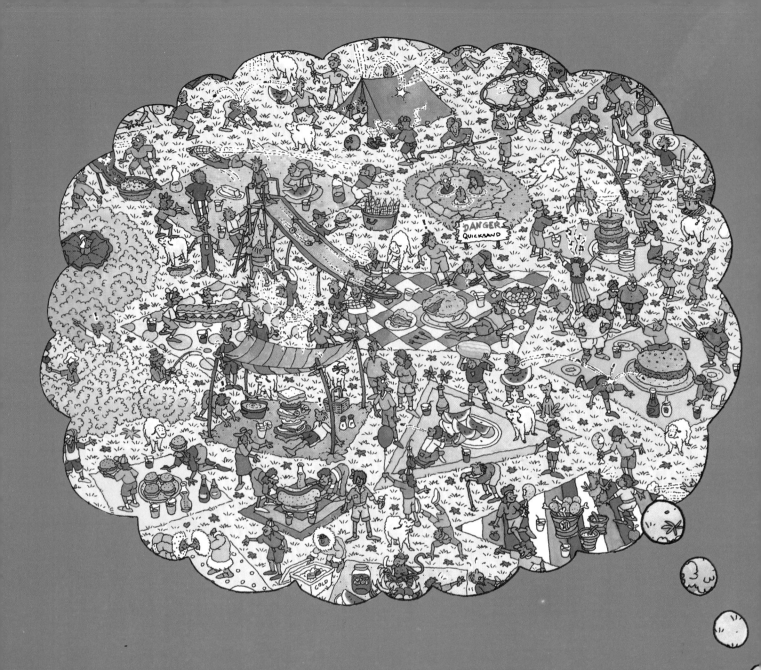

Published in Nashville, Tennessee, by Oliver-Nelson Books, a division of Thomas Nelson, Inc., Publishers, and distributed in Canada by Lawson Falle, Ltd., Cambridge, Ontario.

Printed in the United States of America.

   ISBN 0–8407–9675–7

1 2 3 4 5 6 —98 97 96 95 94 93

SAMMY'S
EXCELLENT
REAL-LIFE
ADVENTURES

It all started because . . .

I am a shepherd boy. I spend many hours taking care of my sheep. It gets pretty lonely out in the fields. I am glad I have a friend to talk with. My friend is younger than I am, so I tell him stories that will teach him to be a good person . . . er, sheep.

Yes, my friend is a sheep named Sammy. But sheep need to be able to get along with one another just like people do.

Sammy sits quietly by my side and listens to me. Just the other day I was telling Sammy some of the ways that a good friend treats others. I know I am just imagining, but it seems like Sammy really wants to learn how to treat others.

Would you like to hear some of the friendship tips I gave Sammy? Great! While you are learning them, see if you can find Sammy and some of my other friends in pictures of some of my favorite places.

Spaceman

Unicycle Mouse

Fisherman

Twin Babies

COURAGEOUS CODY

VISITS THE CIRCUS

Have you ever had to do something that was really scary? Maybe you had to speak in front of a group of people. Maybe you moved and had to go to a new school.

When you have to try something new, you need courage. *Courage* means being brave enough to try something that scares you.

The circus is full of courageous people. Courageous Cody is one of them. Can you find him?

Parting the Red Seats

Eating on the Job

Courageous Cody

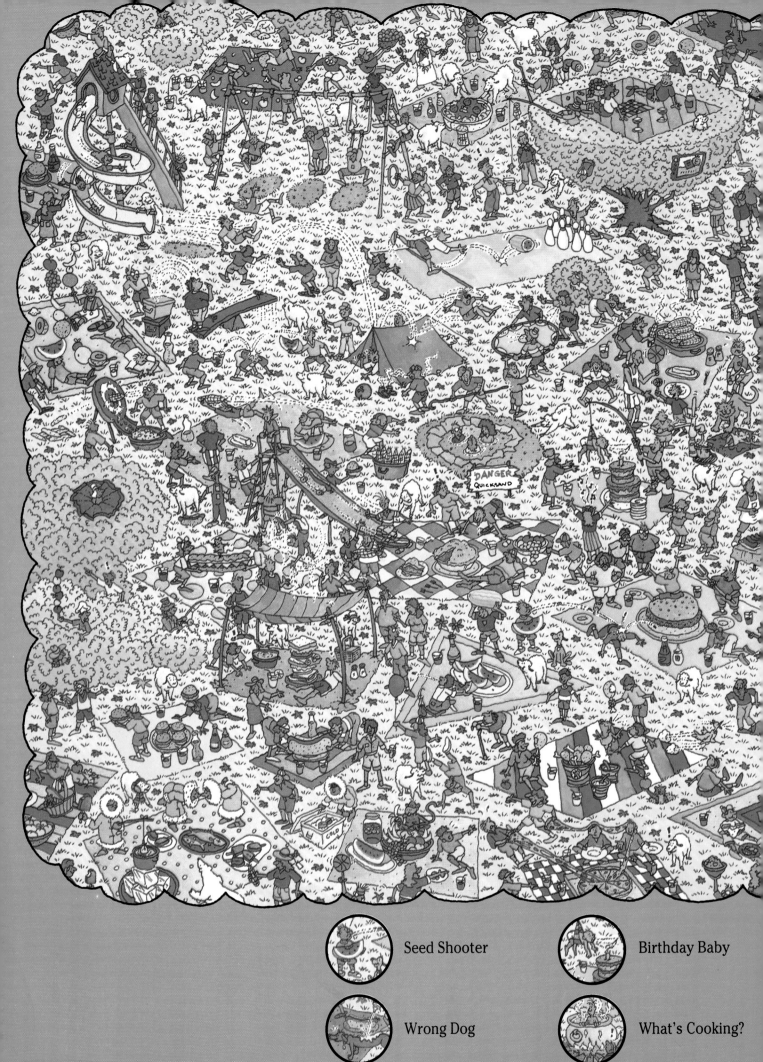

Seed Shooter

Birthday Baby

Wrong Dog

What's Cooking?

SHARIN' KAREN HAS FUN AT THE PICNIC

Sharing means letting a friend hold your new kitten. Sharing means giving half your lunch to a friend who forgot to bring one. Sharing means letting someone have a turn on your favorite swing.

You feel good when a friend shares with you. You can make a friend feel good by sharing what you have and what you do.

See if you can find my special friend Sharin' Karen sharing with someone at the picnic.

Upset Chicken

Stinky Shoes

Sharin' Karen

 Got the Point

 Totally Cool

 Fast Food

 Sheepdog

RUTH THE TRUTH
RIDES THE WATERSLIDE

Have you ever known people you could not trust? They might tell you something, but you would not know whether or not it was true.

Being around someone who tells lies is not pleasant. Lies can hurt other people and make them sad. It is best to tell the *truth* always with kindness.

Ruth the Truth always tells the truth, but she does not hurt her friends' feelings. She is gentle with the truth. Can you find her at the water park?

Robin's Good!

Touch-Up-Side Down

Ruth the Truth

Taco-to-Go

Ticket Taker

Missing Dart

Fish Dinner
for Two

GRATEFUL GREGORY

DISCOVERS THE CARNIVAL

When your mom or dad makes dinner for you, do you take time to say, "Thank you"? You reach in your drawer and pull out clean socks. Do you thank the person who did your laundry? Are you *grateful* for the things people do for you? Are you grateful for the family and home that God gave you? Do not forget to say, "Thank you!"

Grateful Gregory is thankful for everything he has. Can you find him at the carnival?

Sherlock's Son

Sheep Shooter

Grateful Gregory

Tree Topper

Traveling
Salesman

Slingshot

Pan Fish

FAITHFUL FREDDIE
ENJOYS DOWNHILL SKIING

Good friends are *faithful*. That means you can count on them. Faithful people say nice things about their friends when their friends are not around. They stick with their buddies even when their buddies hurt their feelings.

Faithful people make new friends without forgetting their old ones. You can trust a loyal, faithful friend.

Faithful Freddie told some friends he would meet them on the slopes. Can you find him there?

Real Hands–On Skier

Magic Carpet Ride

Faithful Freddie

 Is That My Ball?

 You'll Be Sorry

 Strong Shoes

 High Tech Golf

JOYFUL JASON
PLAYS MINIATURE GOLF

A *joyful* person is happy to be alive. A joyful person is delighted with family and friends and can see the good in a situation instead of always looking at the bad side.

A joyful person usually has more friends than a grumpy person.

Joyful Jason is playing miniature golf today. Can you find him? Is he showing any joy today?

Say What?

Out of the Rough

Joyful Jason

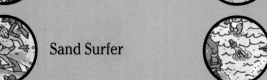

Jammin' Sheep

Water–Ski Mouse

Sand Surfer

Message in a Bottle

DILIGENT DANNY
GETS THE JOB DONE AT THE BEACH

When you are cleaning your room, emptying trash cans for your mom, doing homework, or working a puzzle, you should do your best to finish the project. That means you are being diligent.

Diligence is sticking with something until you have finished the project, even if it takes a long time. Finally finishing a hard puzzle is very satisfying.

Look at the picture of kids playing at the beach. My friend Diligent Danny is at the beach today. See if you can find him finishing a project.

No Snow

Bad Bump

Diligent Danny

Unplugged

Spare Ribs

Not a Happy Camper

Man with Taco

PATIENT PETER

WAITS HIS TURN
AT THE
CAMP FIRE

Waiting is hard. It is hard to wait for your friends to play the game you want to play. It is hard to wait your turn at the water fountain. It is even hard to wait for your parents to listen to what you want to tell them. When people are good at waiting, we call them *patient*.

Patient Peter has learned to wait. He is being patient at the camp fire. Can you find him?

Char Dog

Tune A. Fish

Patient Peter

Emergency
Phone Call

One Little Piggy

Amateur
Musician

Bold Boxer Shorts

HUMBLE HANNA
JOINS THE PARADE

Do you know people who are really smart or who have beautiful singing voices? If they brag about how good they are, you might not enjoy being around them. If they do not brag, they are being *humble*. Humble people do not tell you how great they are. Humble people do not mind if others are praised or cheered. They are just happy to do what they do and enjoy it.

Humble Hanna never brags. Today she is in a parade. When you find her, you might notice that she is being humble.

Light Lunch

Abe the Sheep

Humble Hanna

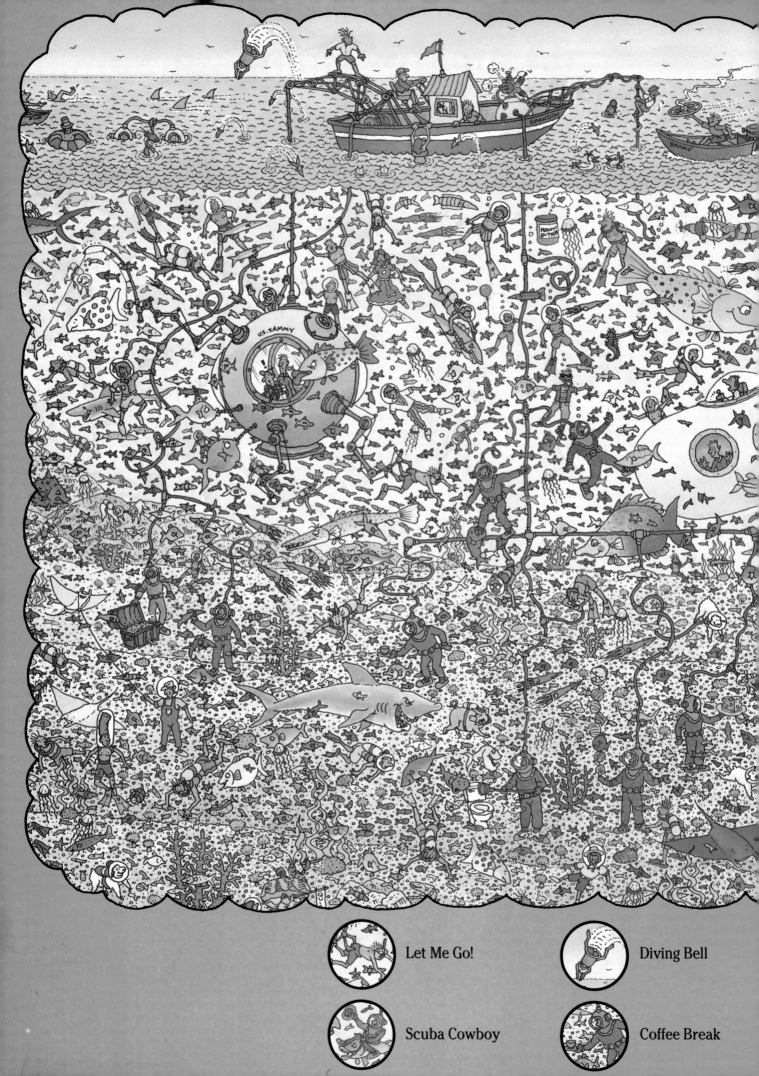

Let Me Go!

Diving Bell

Scuba Cowboy

Coffee Break

COURTEOUS COURTNEY GOES SCUBA DIVING

Being *courteous* means being polite. For example, a courteous person takes turns on the playground swings. A courteous person says, "Excuse me," "Please," and "May I?" A courteous person does not run or shout inside buildings.

Courteous Courtney loves scuba diving. But even when she is doing her favorite thing, she remembers to be courteous. Can you find her?

Wrong Place, Wrong Time

Lunch Selection

Courteous Courtney

 Motor Mouse

 Rocket Racer

 Fishin' Fool

 Ewe-nicycle

HELPFUL HENRY
LENDS A HAND AT THE GO-CART TRACK

Are you good at putting model airplanes together? Can you French-braid hair? Are you better than anyone else at hitting a baseball? If a friend asks for your help with something that you do better than she does, are you willing to do it?

Each of us has a specialty, something that we enjoy doing and are good at. It is fun to be able to *help* a friend do something. You feel needed, and your friend is grateful for your help.

Helpful Henry has a specialty. He is busy at the go-cart track right now using his specialty to help someone. Can you find him?

Ironic Chores

Out of Season

Helpful Henry

 Love Lift Us Up

 Light Snack

 Taken for Granite

 Sky Diver?

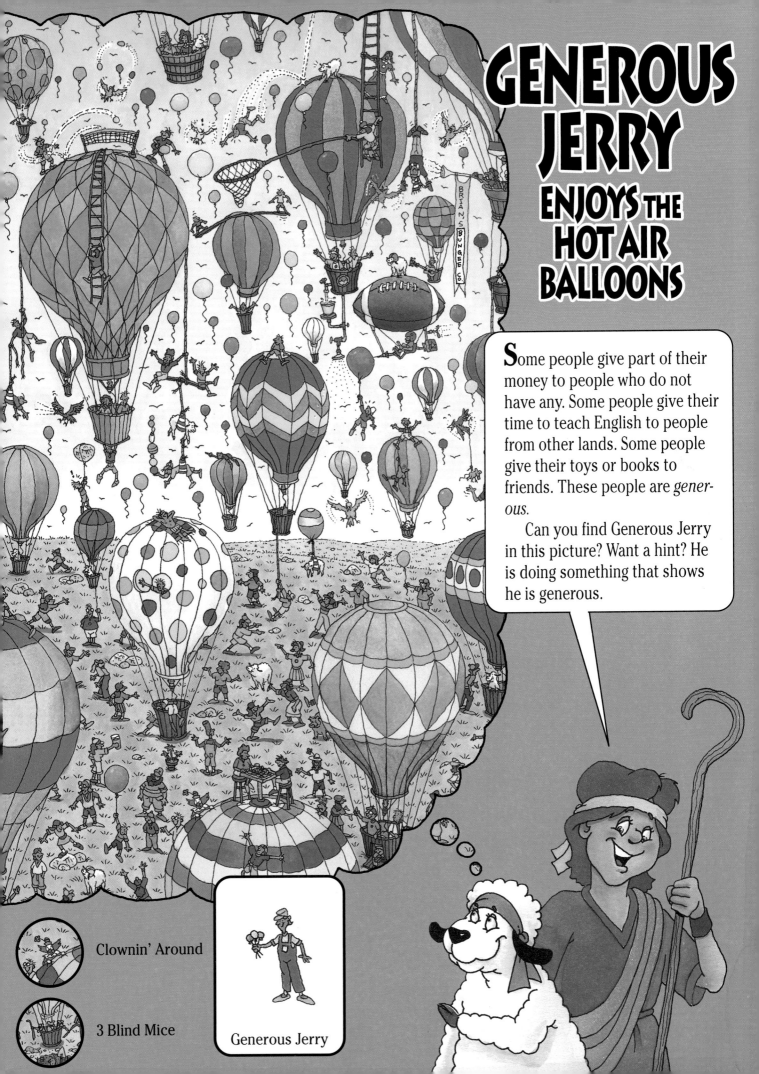

GENEROUS JERRY
ENJOYS THE HOT AIR BALLOONS

Some people give part of their money to people who do not have any. Some people give their time to teach English to people from other lands. Some people give their toys or books to friends. These people are *generous*.

Can you find Generous Jerry in this picture? Want a hint? He is doing something that shows he is generous.

Clownin' Around

3 Blind Mice

Generous Jerry

Shady Character

Kitty Napped

Souvenir Sheep

Whistling Dickie

KIND CHRISTINA
SPENDS A DAY AT THE ZOO

A *kind* person is gentle and friendly. A kind person cares about others' feelings. You show kindness by the way you speak to your brother or sister. You show kindness by the way you treat your pets. You show kindness by your tone of voice when you speak with others. Kind people make others want to be kind.

Kind Christina is at the zoo. She is probably doing something that shows how kind she is. Can you find her?

The Muffin Man

Walkin' the Dog

Kind Christina

SEEKING SAMMY

See how many of **the shepherd boy's friends** you can find—all 13 are in each picture.
Then see how many **crazy things** you can find from the lists below:

COURAGEOUS CODY VISITS THE CIRCUS
1. Egg Thrower
2. Fish on Unicycle
3. Cowboy Clown
4. Dog
5. Sheep Family
6. Firefighter
7. Mouse Juggler
8. Bag of Peanuts
9. Sheep with Sunglasses
10. Native American Blowing Bubbles
11. Strong Mouse

SHARIN' KAREN HAS FUN AT THE PICNIC
1. Spaghetti and Meatballs
2. Mustard Gun
3. Alarm Clock
4. Mouse on Sub
5. Taco
6. Monkey with Banana
7. Corn Catcher
8. 10–Foot Hot Dog
9. Giant Sundae
10. Bucket of Barbecue Sauce
11. Water Fountain

RUTH THE TRUTH RIDES THE WATERSLIDE
1. Man Reading Book
2. Rabbit
3. Mouse in Kayak
4. Smelly Sneaker
5. Giraffe
6. Fishbowl
7. Juggling Monkey
8. Boy on Hook
9. Lion
10. Umbrella
11. Donkey

GRATEFUL GREGORY DISCOVERS THE CARNIVAL
1. Boy with Bubble Gum
2. Watermelon for 2
3. 3–Foot Hot Dog
4. Boom Box
5. Overdressed Man
6. Singing Sheep
7. Football Players
8. Man with Rocket Pack
9. Doughnut Balloon
10. Taco
11. Bone in Man's Beard

FAITHFUL FREDDIE ENJOYS DOWNHILL SKIING
1. Frozen Fish
2. Runaway Bathtub
3. 3–Person Skis
4. Ski Boat
5. Rocket Man
6. Man on Inline Skates
7. Snow Cones for Sale
8. Flower Garden
9. Sunbather
10. Drummer on Skis
11. Book

JOYFUL JASON PLAYS MINIATURE GOLF
1. Overdressed Man
2. Slice of Blueberry Pie
3. Firefighter
4. Woman with Very Long Hair
5. Bowler
6. Fruit Bowl Hat
7. 3–Person Putter
8. Tightrope Walker
9. Sunbather
10. Turtle
11. Manhole
12. Baby in Diaper

DILIGENT DANNY GETS THE JOB DONE AT THE BEACH
1. Flying Carpet
2. Lost Skaters
3. Toy Train
4. Blindfolded Head Bangers
5. Shark Imposters
6. Boom Box
7. Goat
8. Sheep Surfer
9. Man in Bath
10. Swordfish
11. 3 Carrots

PATIENT PETER WAITS HIS TURN AT THE CAMP FIRE
1. Tightrope Mouse
2. Bucket of Wieners
3. Flying Bat
4. Hot Feet
5. Running Turtle
6. Mustard and Catsup
7. Handcuffed Hot Dogs
8. Mud Hole Man
9. Sub Sandwich
10. Football
11. Stinky Boots

HUMBLE HANNA JOINS THE PARADE
1. Photographer
2. Cannonball Catcher
3. Sheep with Fan on Head
4. Bungee Jumper
5. Sheep Reading Book
6. Mustard Squirter
7. Man in Barrel
8. Man with Fog Mask
9. Sheep Blowing Bubbles
10. Pirate
11. Woman in Rollers

COURTEOUS COURTNEY GOES SCUBA DIVING
1. Mouse Sub
2. 2 Thirsty Fish
3. Treasure Chest
4. Mermaid
5. Lobster Drummer
6. Peanut Butter and Jelly Love
7. Sawfish
8. Hot Dog Fish
9. Yelling Fish
10. Fishbowl
11. 2 Bone Heads

HELPFUL HENRY LENDS A HAND AT THE GO-CART TRACK
1. On Road Bath
2. 3–Person Car
3. Pit Stop
4. Ice Cream Bar
5. Inline Skater
6. Watermelon on Wheels
7. Umbrella
8. Spiderweb
9. Catsup Cart
10. 10–Scoop Cone
11. Man with Binoculars

GENEROUS JERRY ENJOYS THE HOT AIR BALLOONS
1. Yo-Yo Man
2. Guitar Man
3. Whistler
4. Game of Checkers
5. Baby in Diaper
6. Yelling Sheep
7. Light Bulb
8. Hole Digger
9. Egg Juggler
10. Birdman
11. Pink Pig

KIND CHRISTINA SPENDS A DAY AT THE ZOO
1. Boy on Pogo Stick
2. Man Reading Book
3. Sheep with Balloon
4. Whistler
5. Phone
6. Clown
7. Box of Popcorn
8. Noisy Seal
9. Shovel
10. Hungry Turtle
11. Yo-Yo Man